BLUE

by Melanie Mitchell

first step nonfiction

Lerner Publications Company · Minneapolis

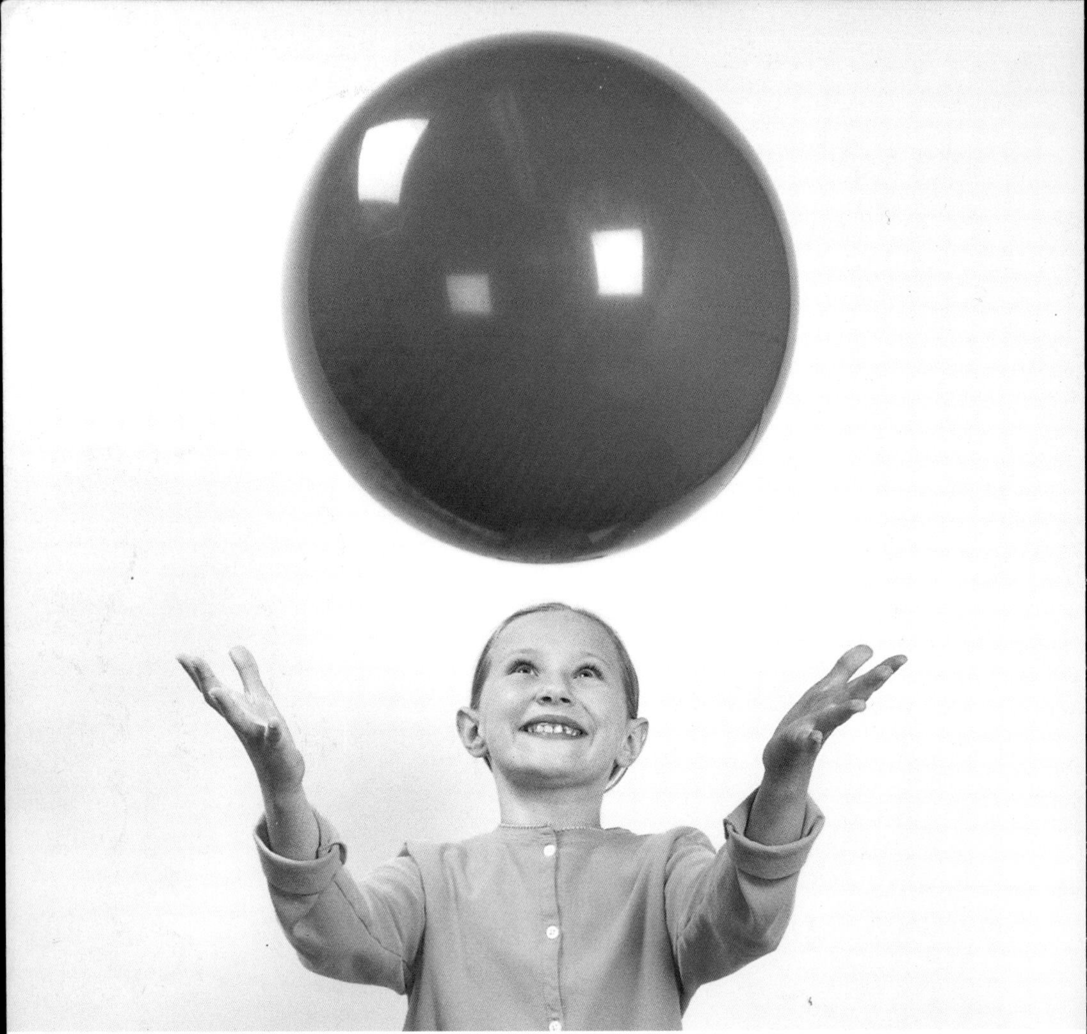

I see blue.

The sky is blue.

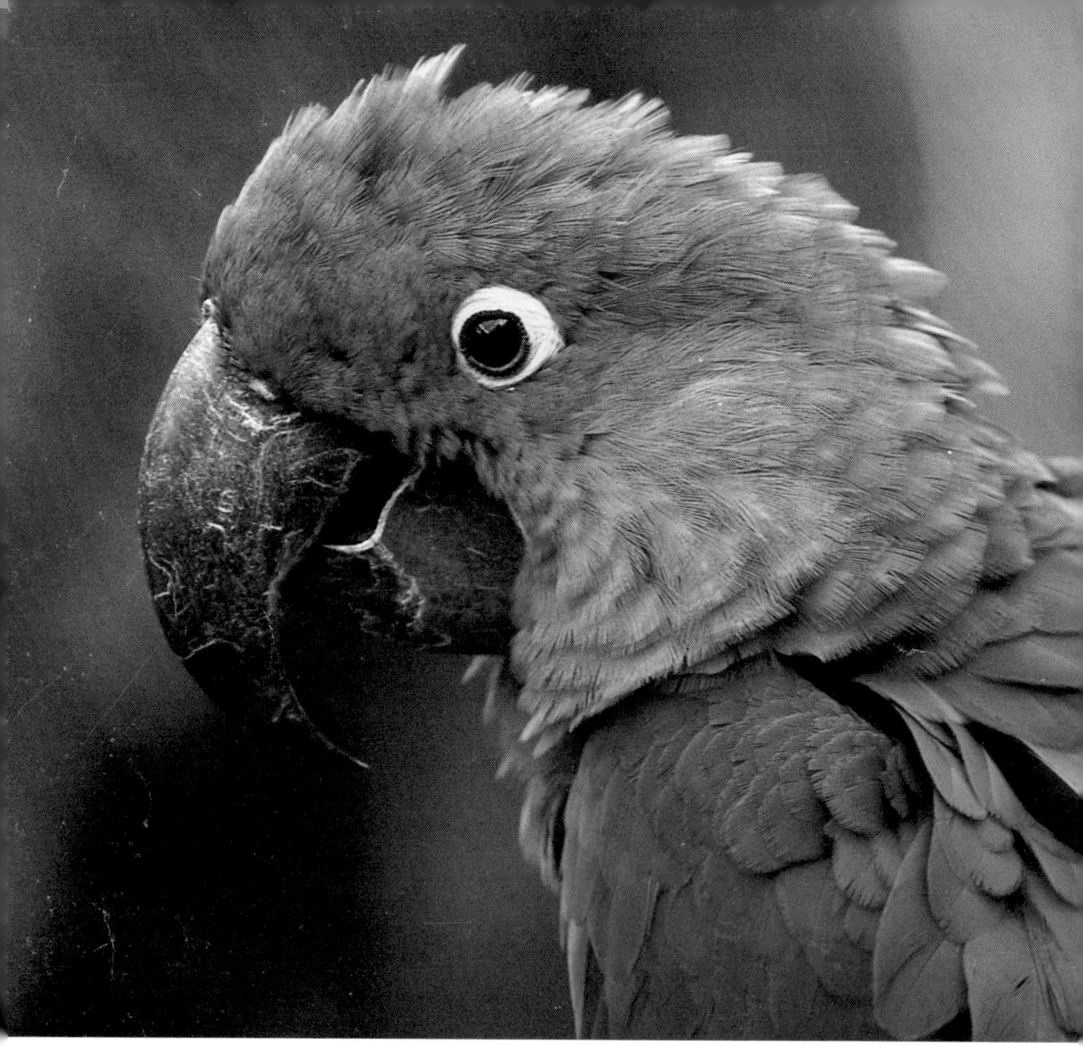

The bird is blue.

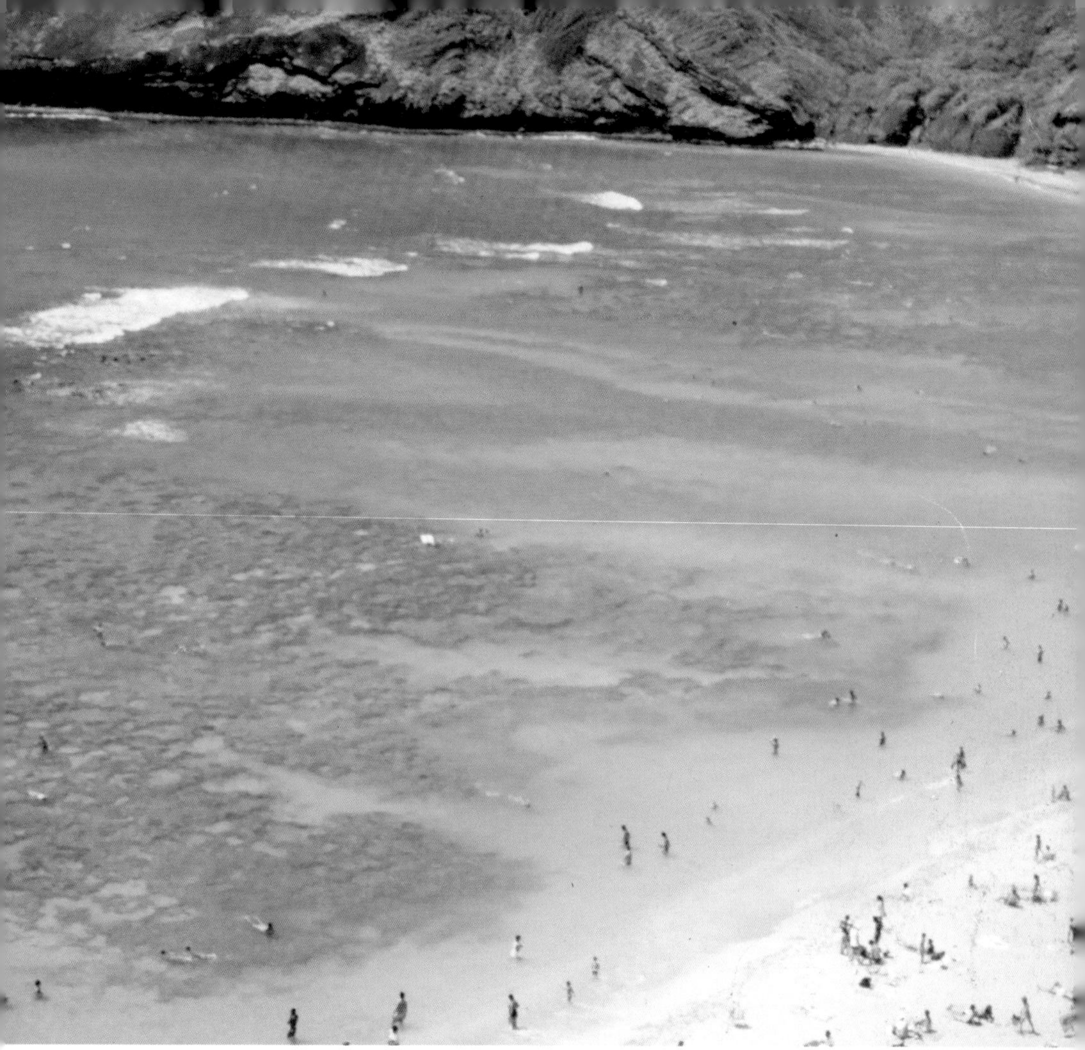

The water is blue.

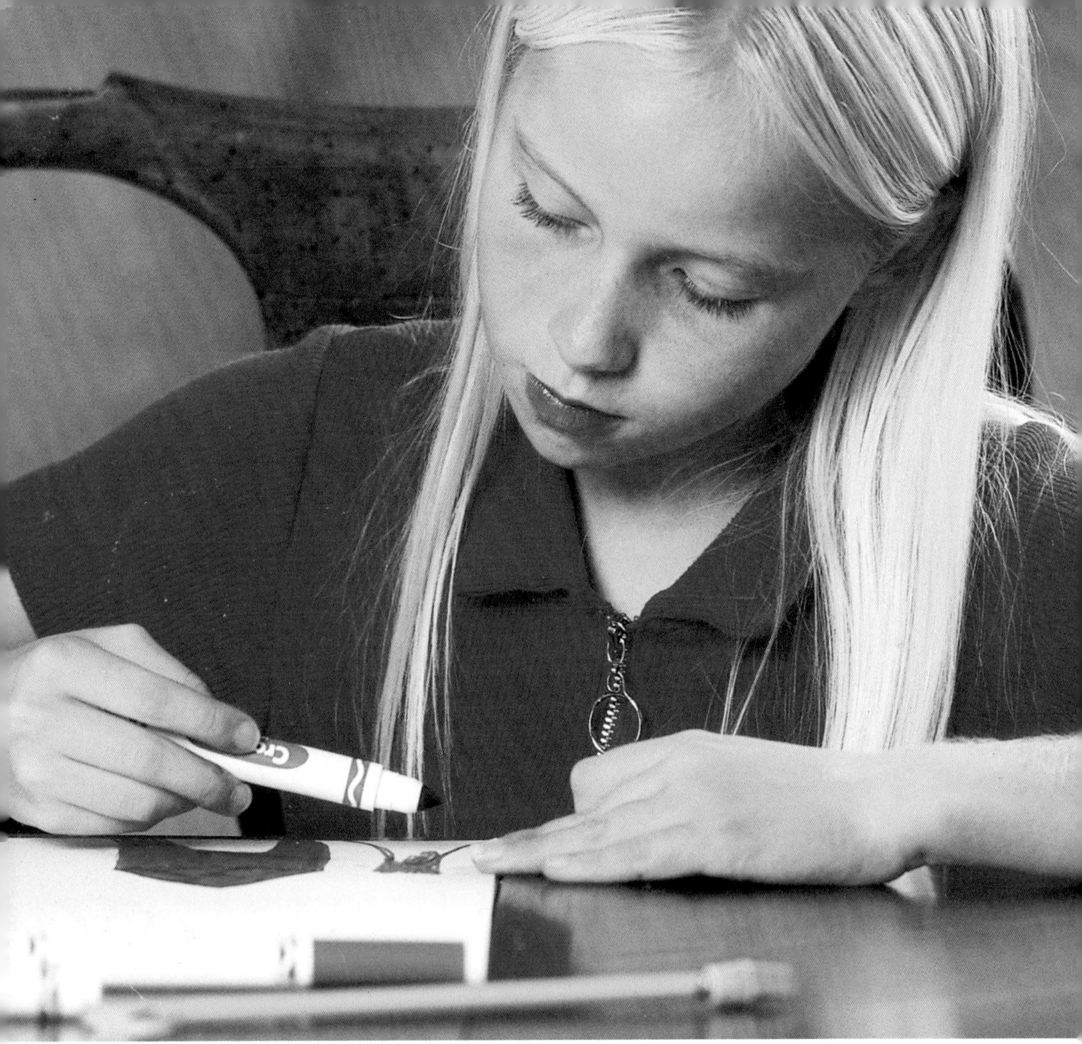

The marker is blue.

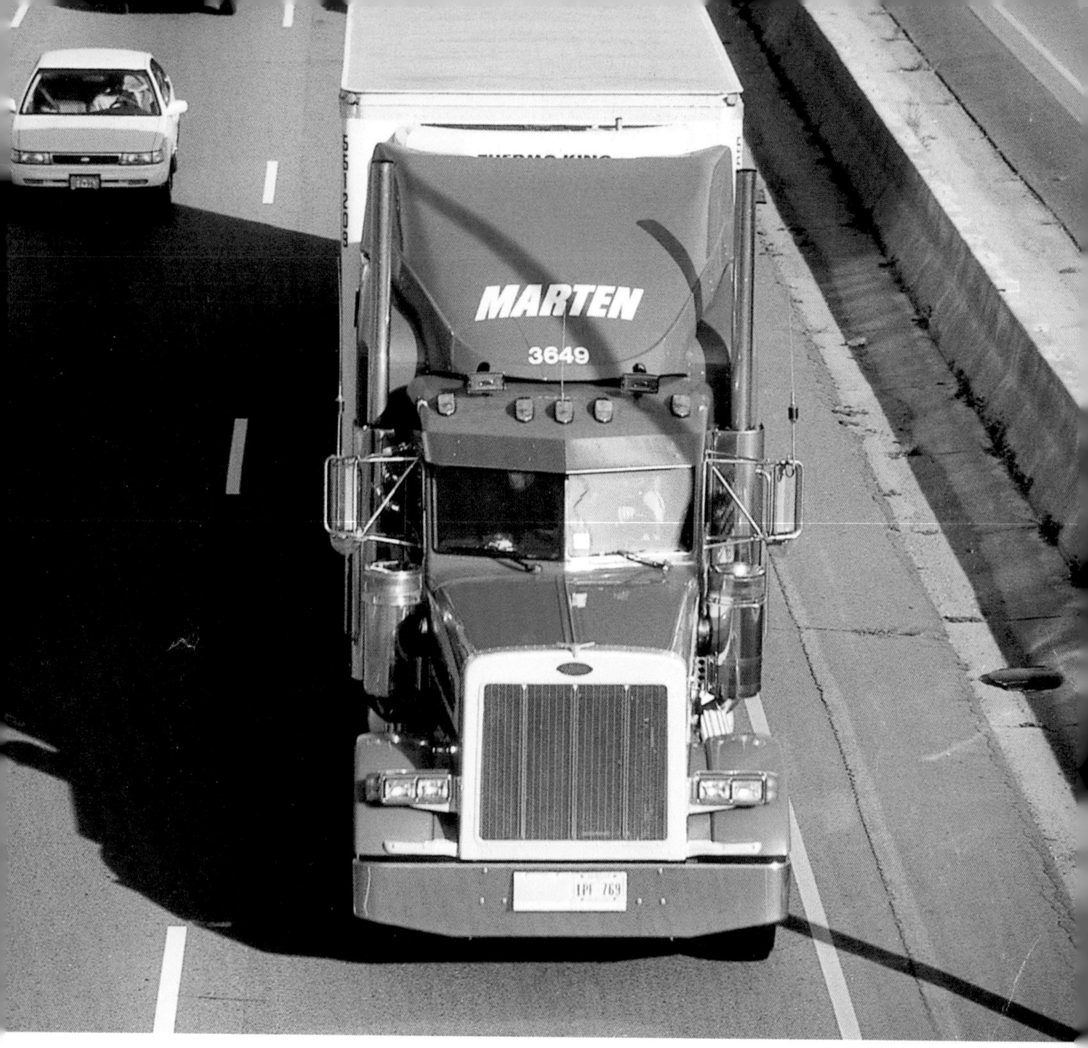

The truck is blue.

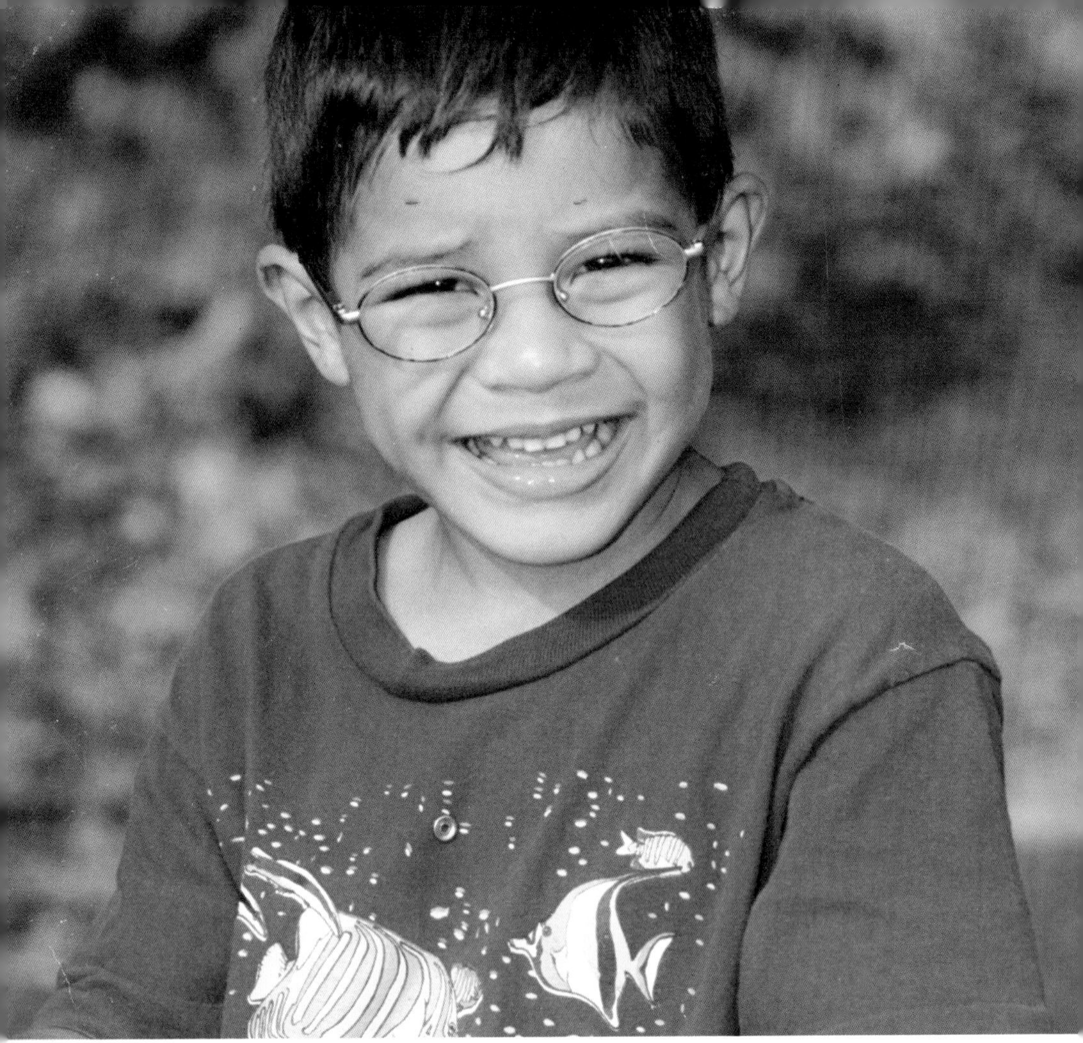

I like blue!